I0467595

Beginners Guide Book To Drawing Vehicles

Your Guide To Drawing Vehicles
The Easy Way

Vehicle Book

By : Gala Publication

Published By :

Gala Publication

© Copyright 2015 – Gala Publication

ISBN-13: **978-1522721642**
ISBN-10: **1522721649**

Table of Contents

AEROPLANE

STEP 1

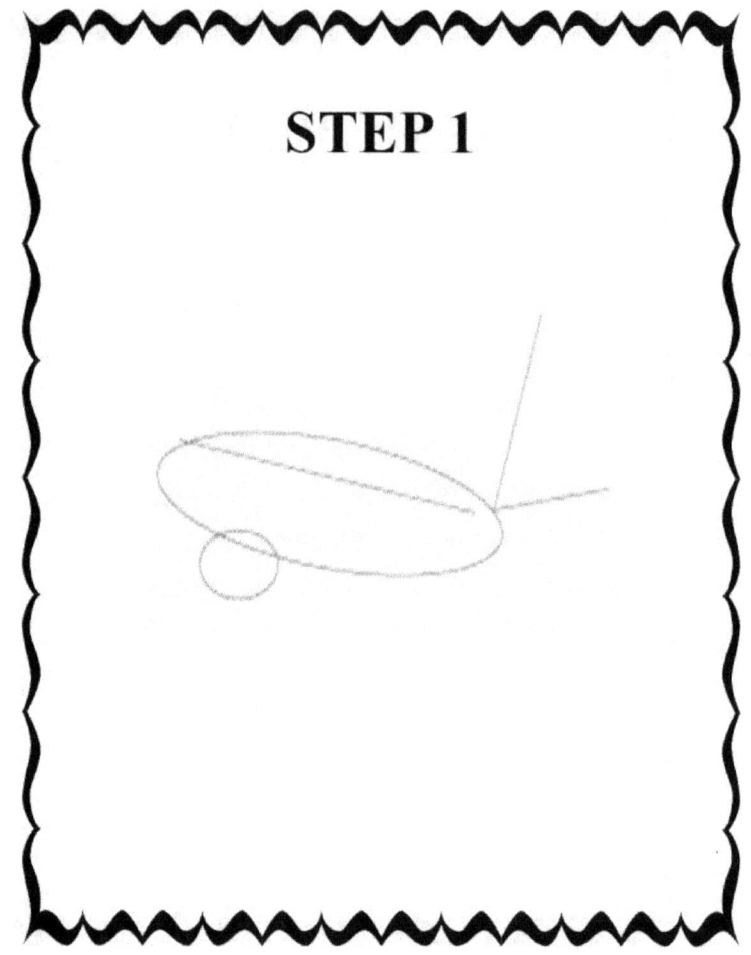

STEP 2

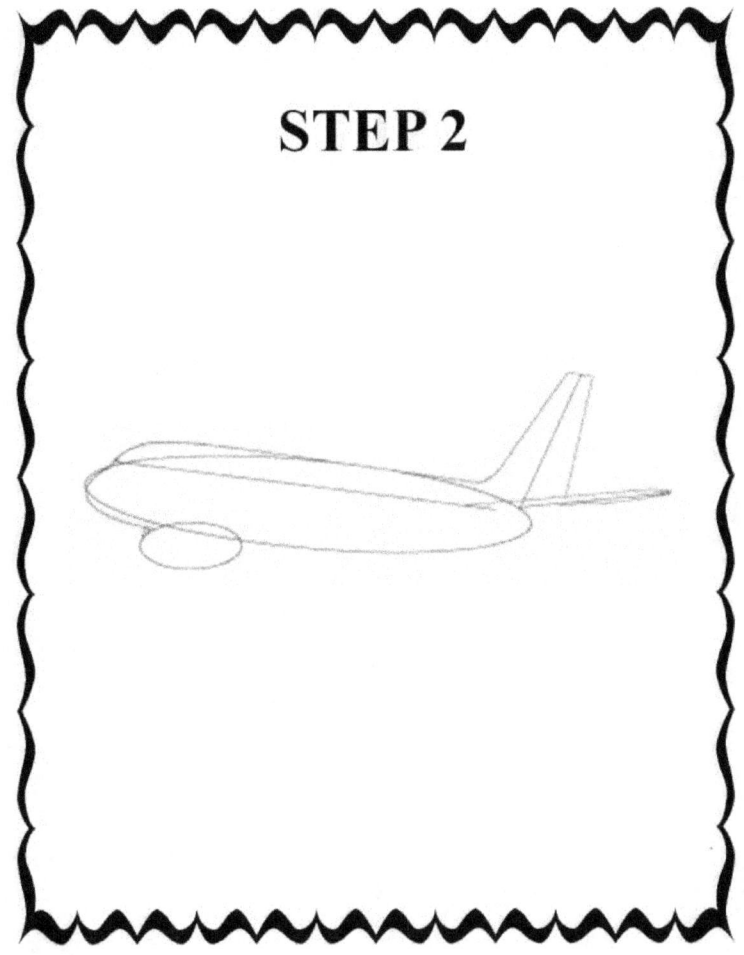

STEP 3

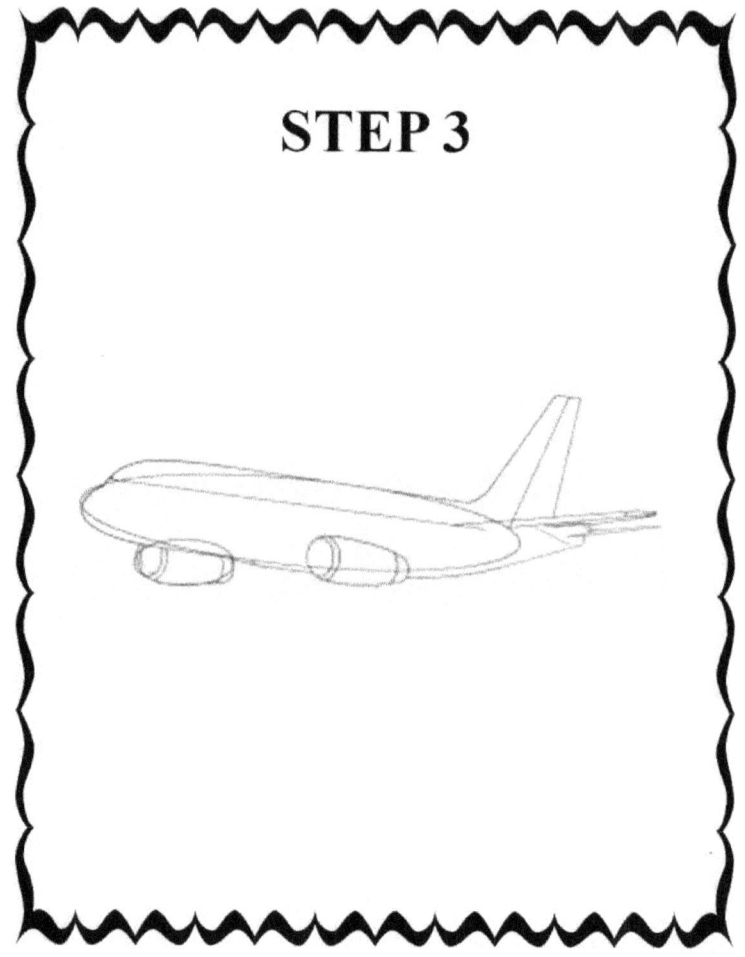

STEP 4

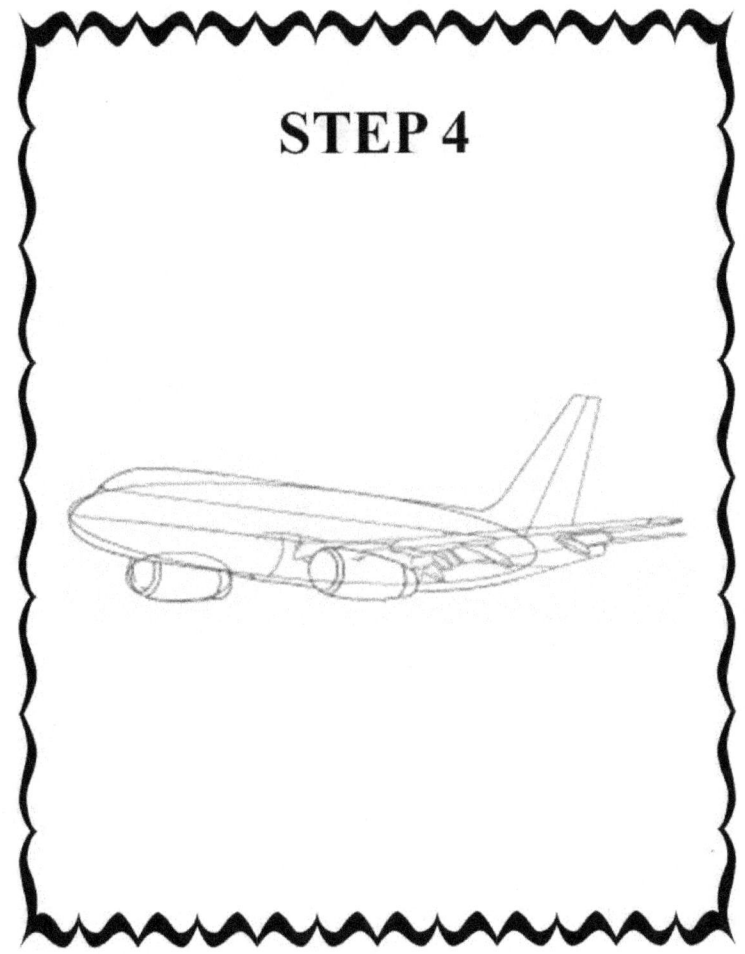

STEP 5

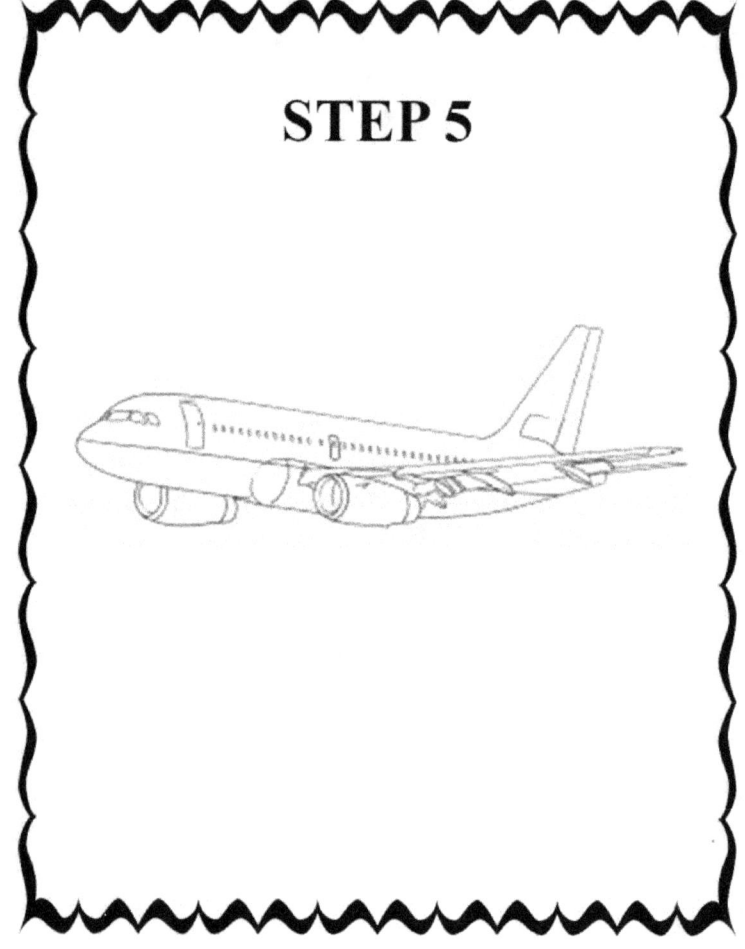

AIRCRAFT

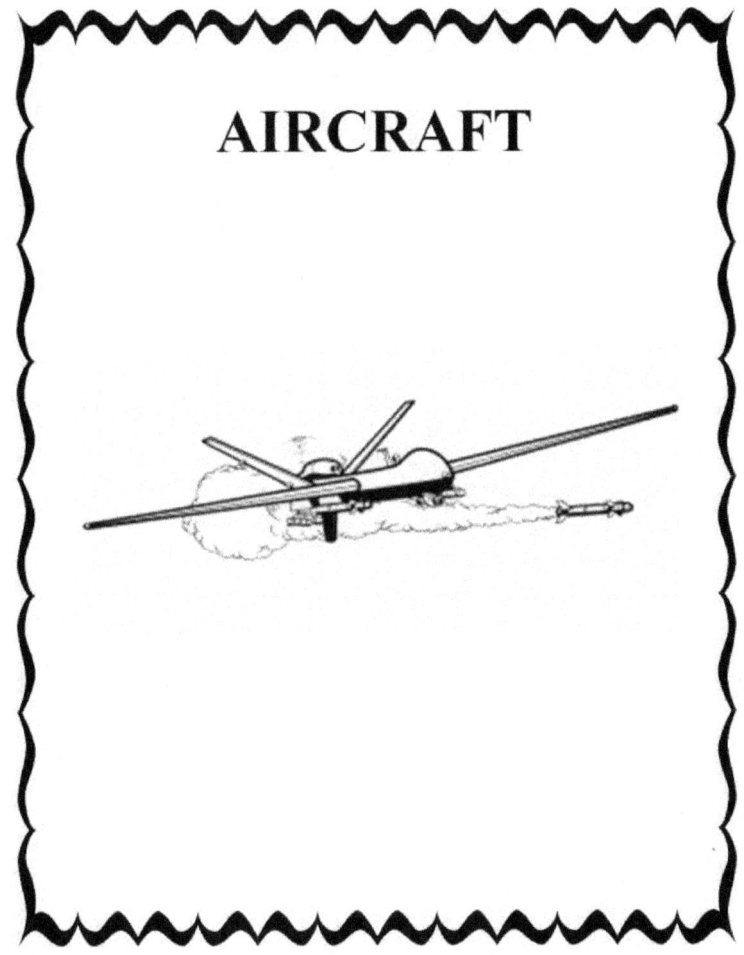

STEP 1

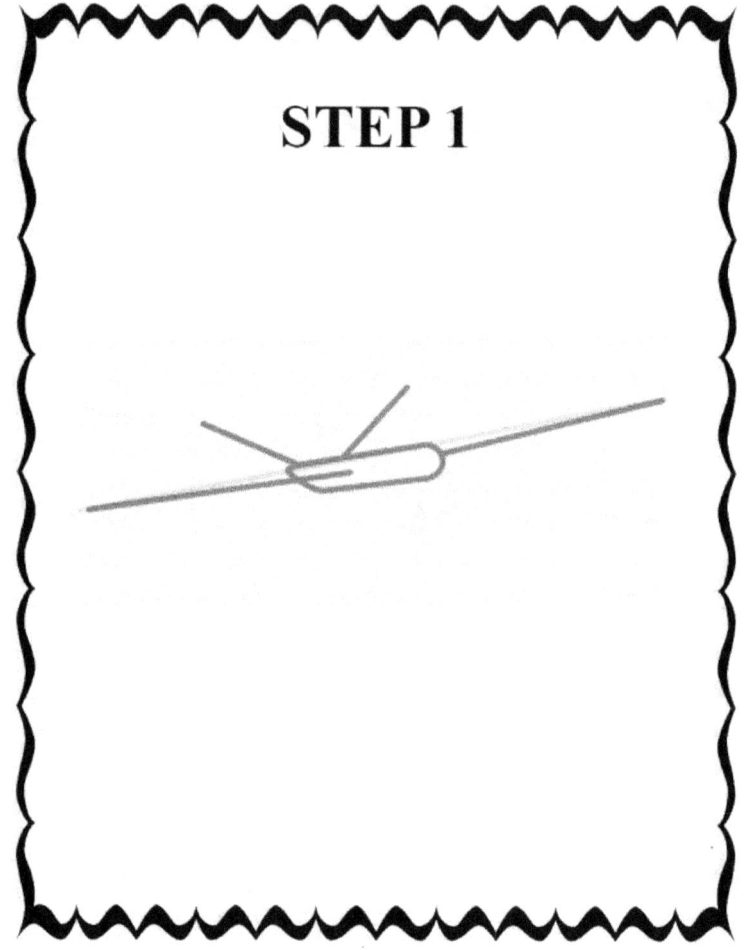

STEP 2

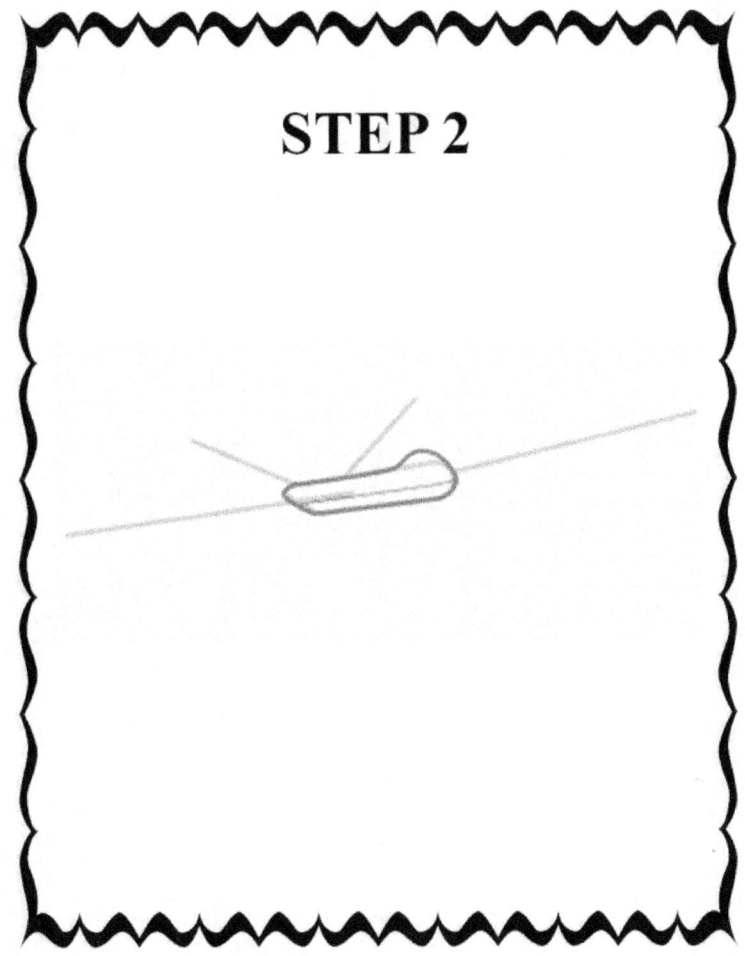

STEP 3

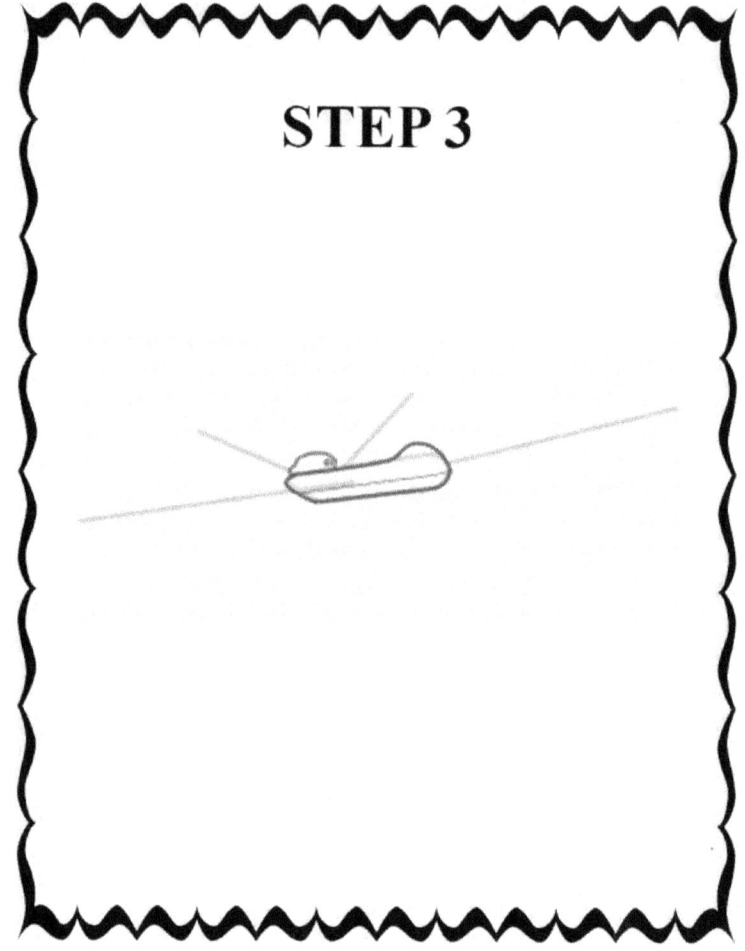

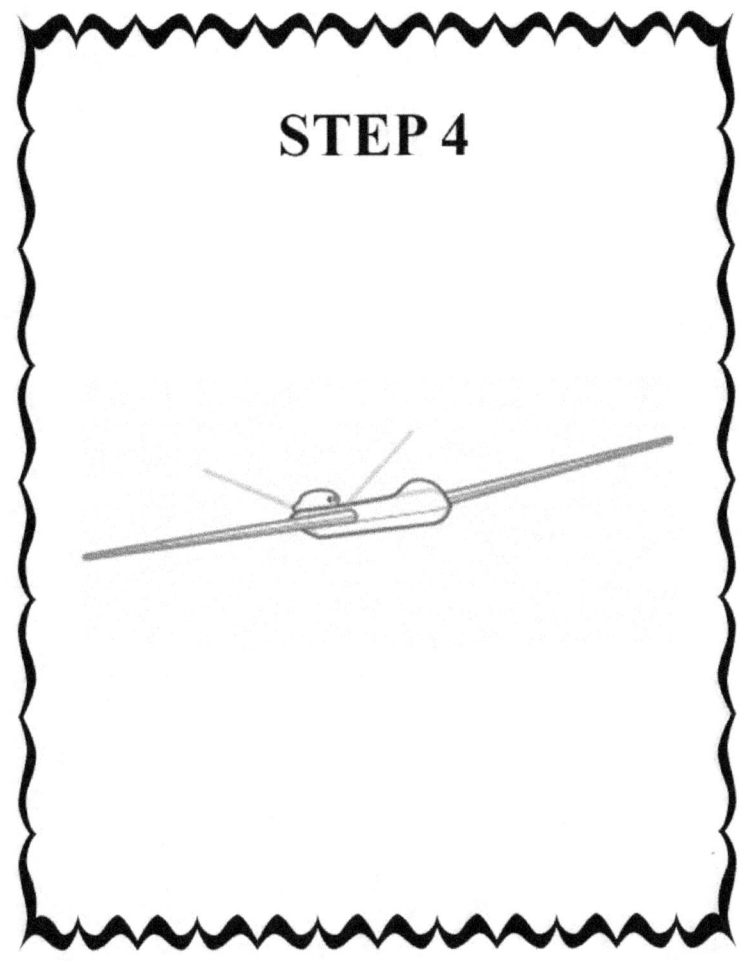

STEP 4

STEP 5

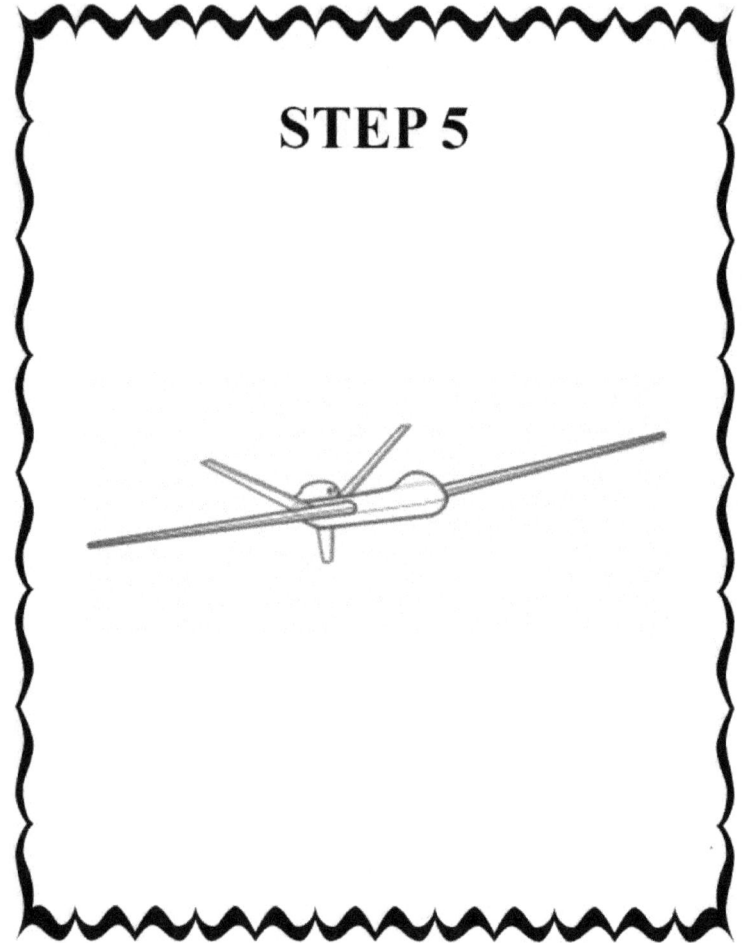

STEP 6

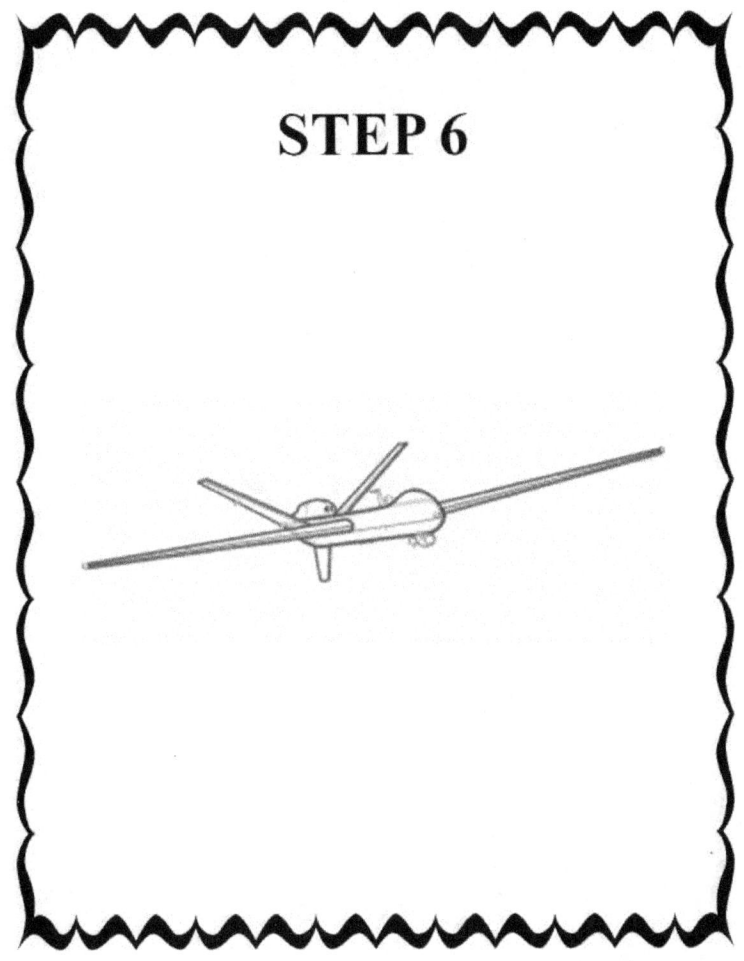

STEP 7

STEP 8

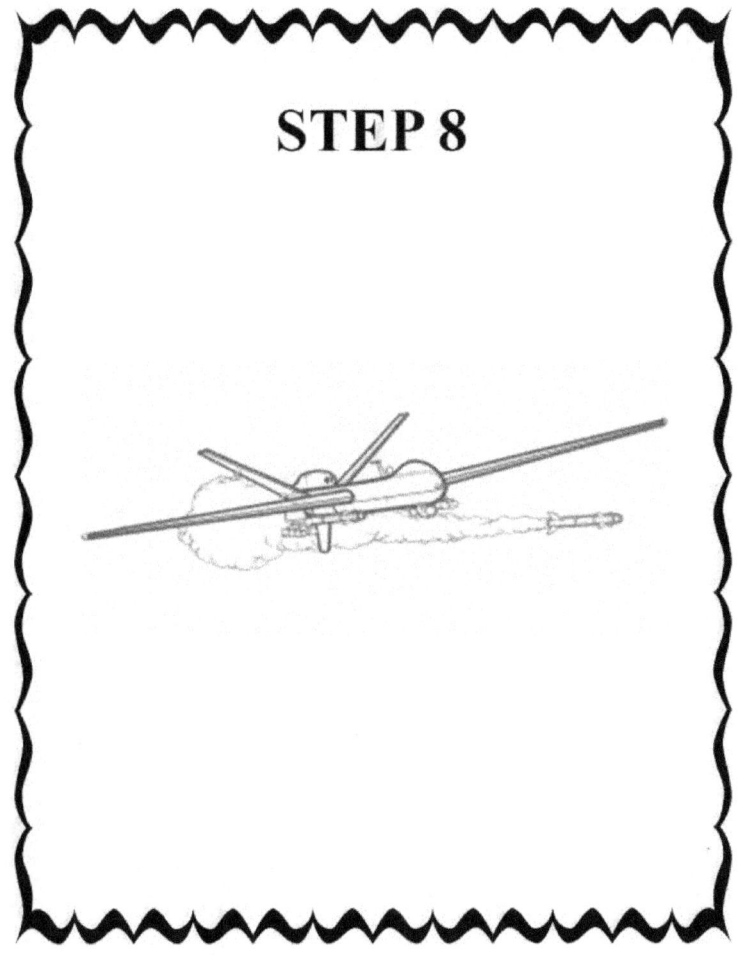

STEP 9

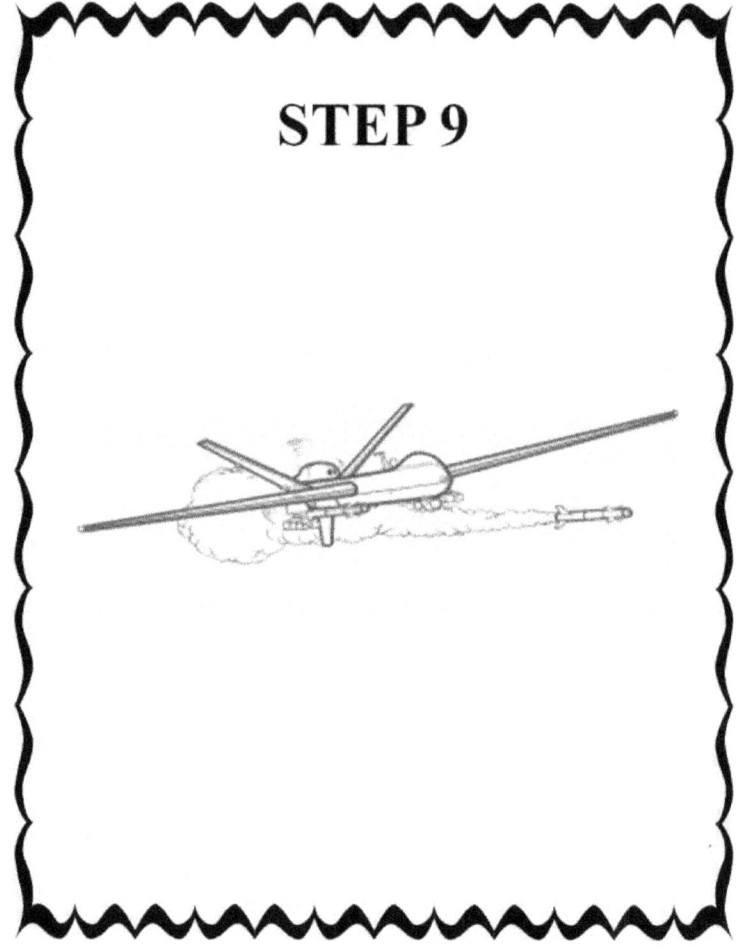

STEP 10

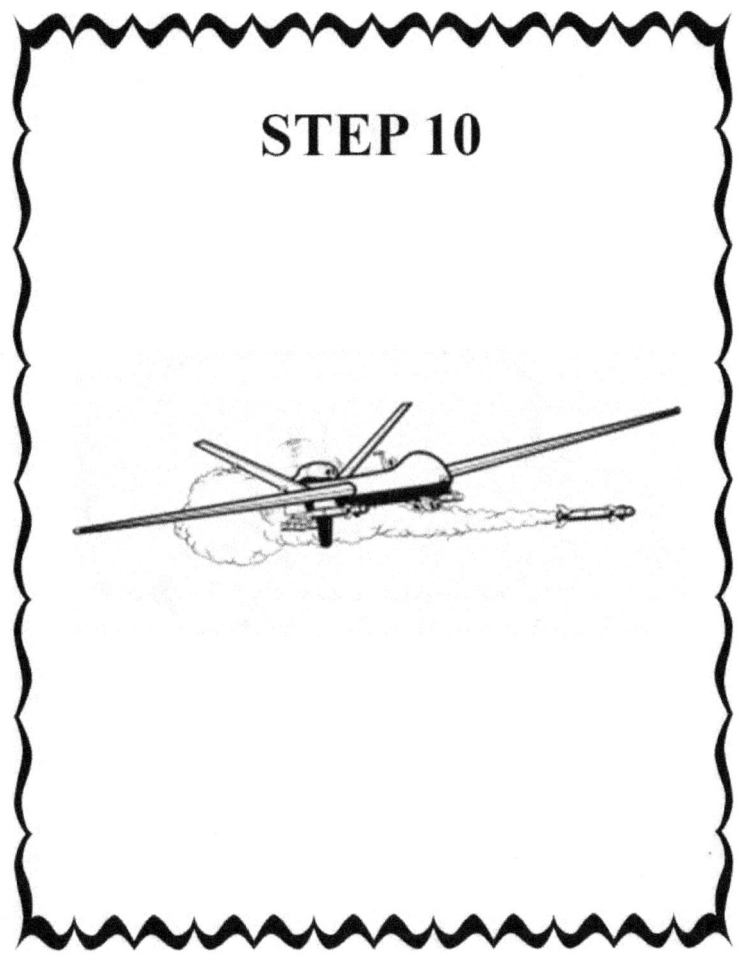

BUS

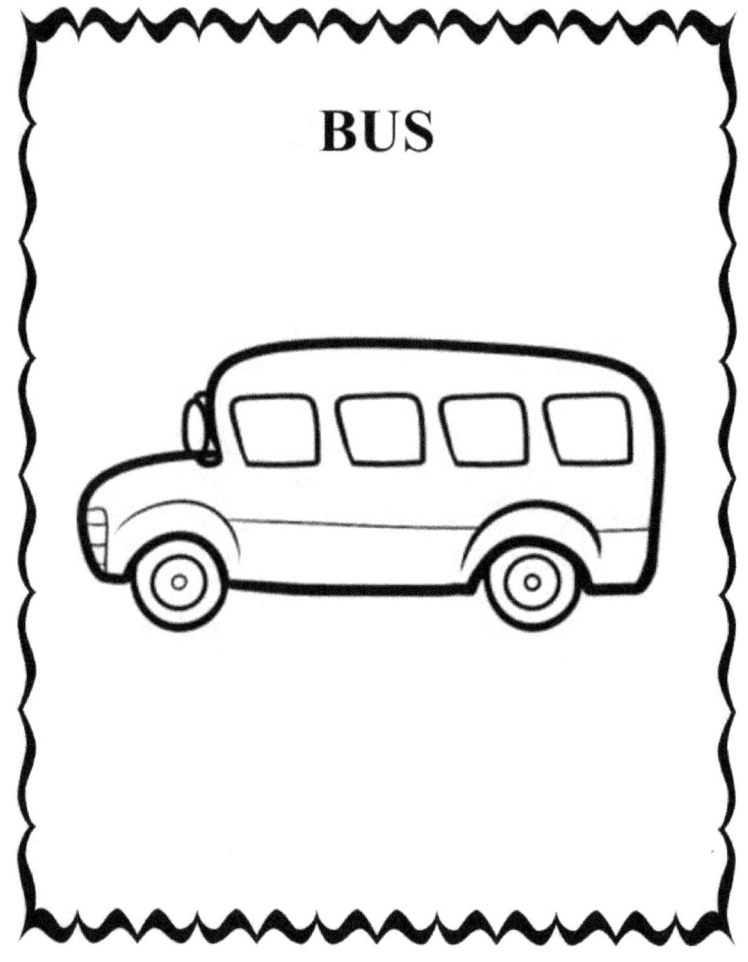

STEP 1

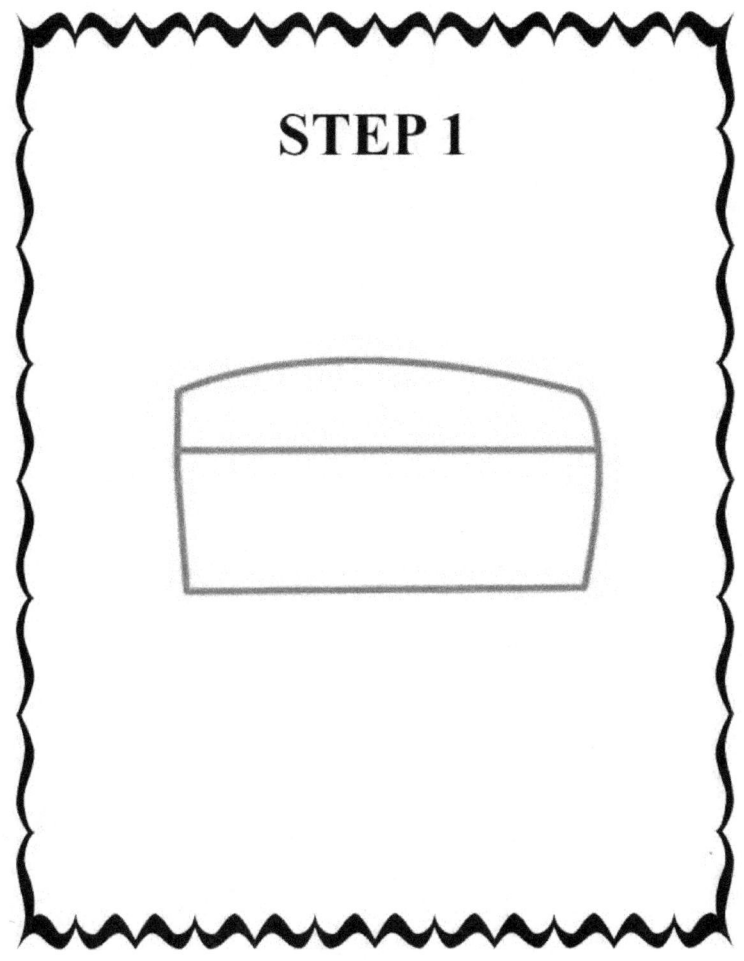

STEP 2

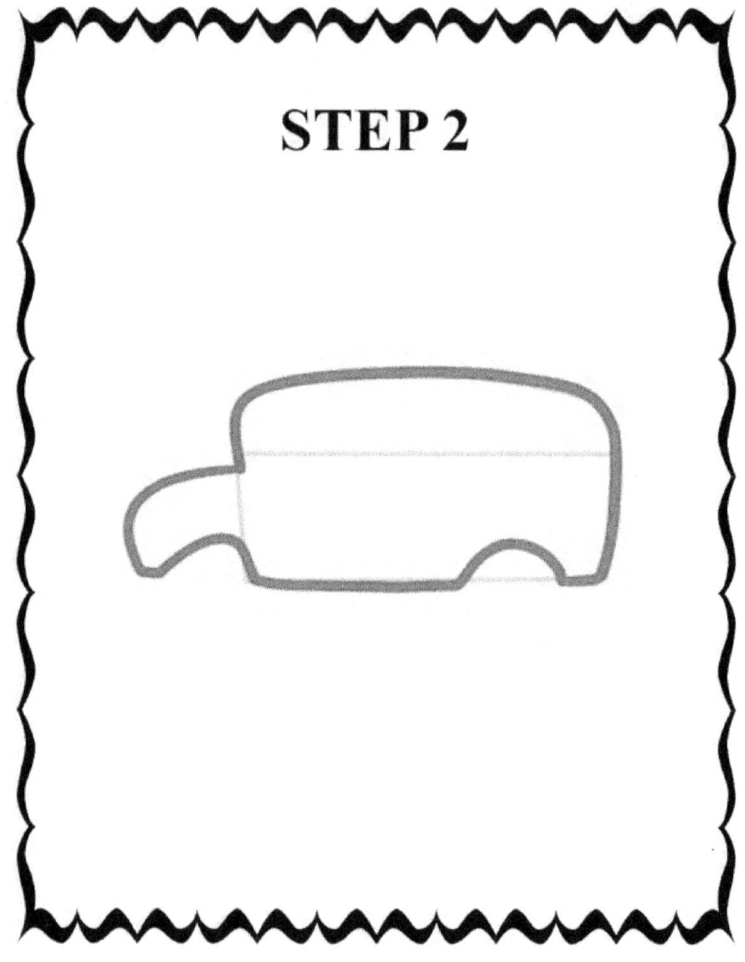

STEP 3

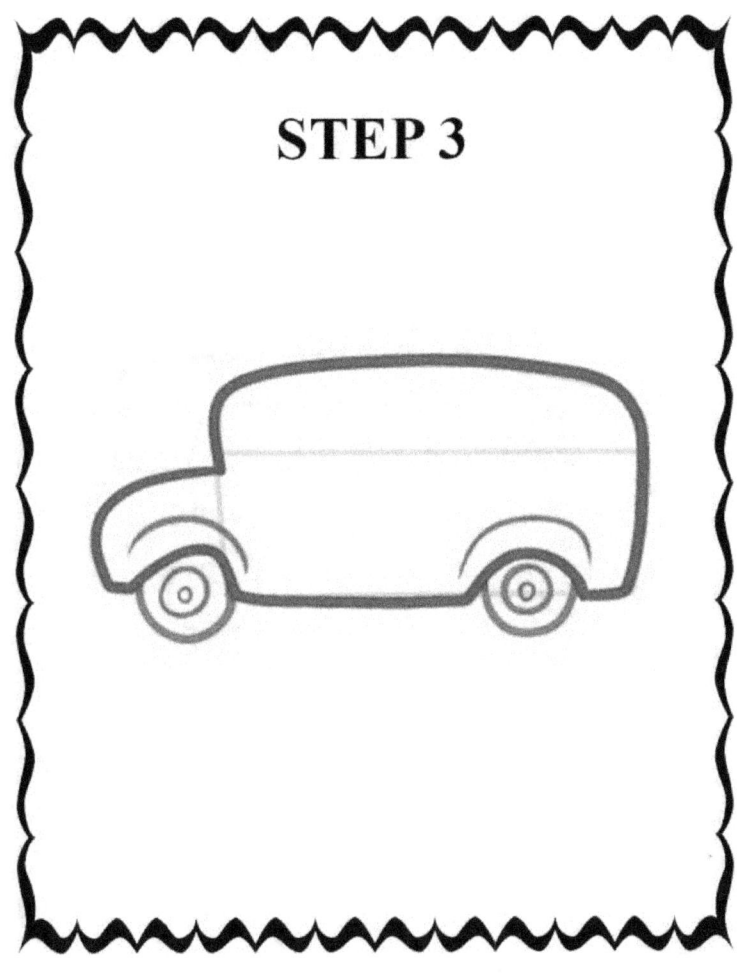

STEP 4

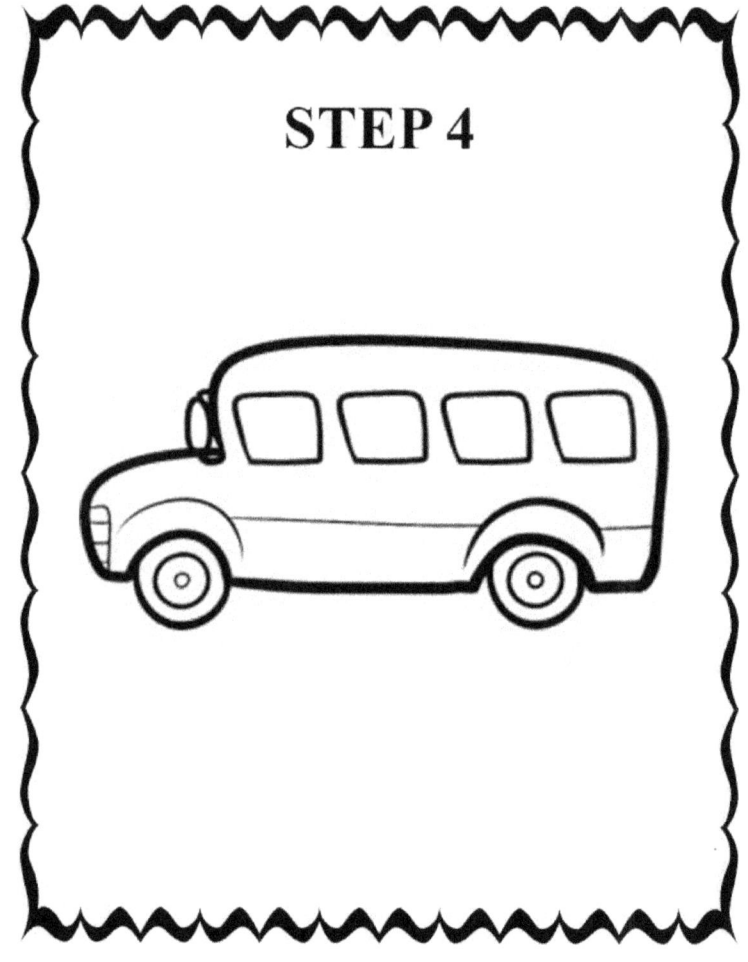

SABER

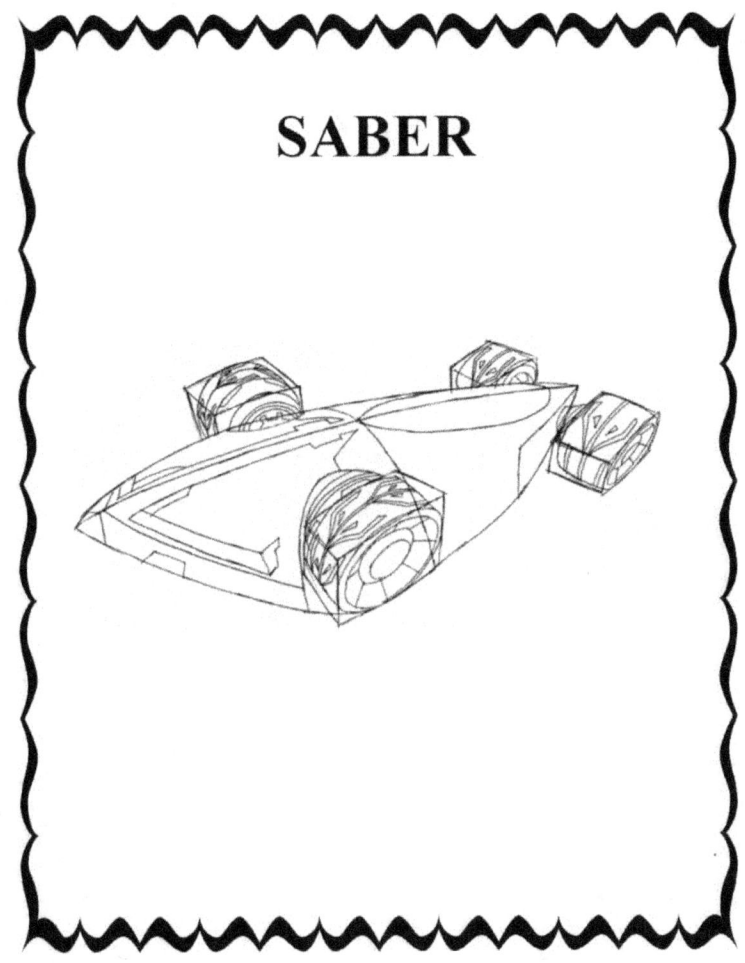

STEP 1

STEP 2

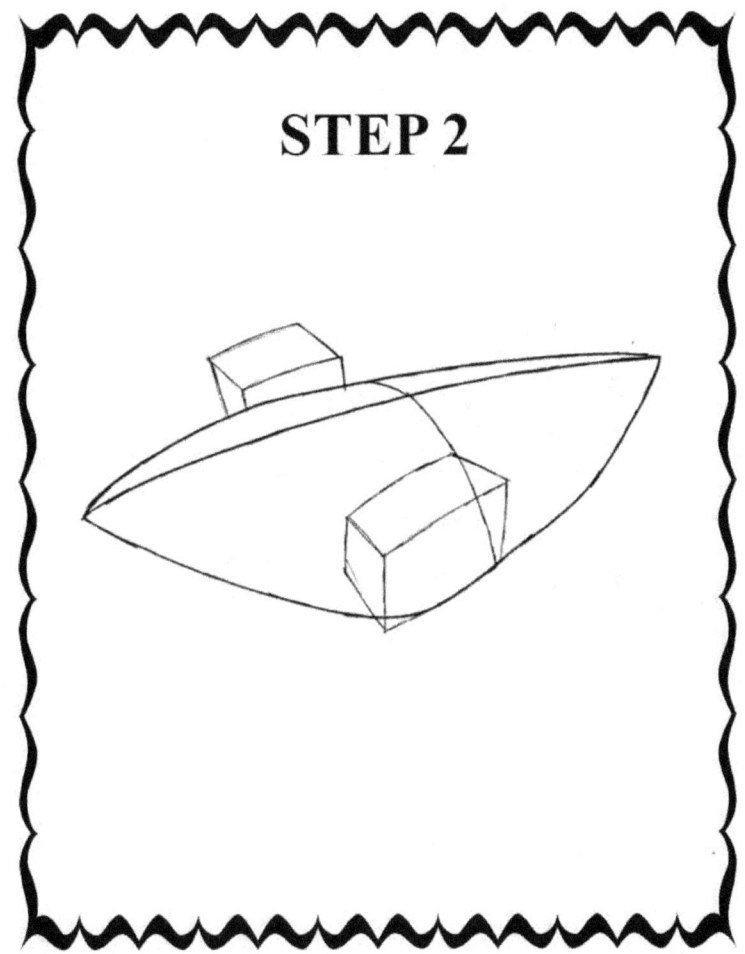

STEP 3

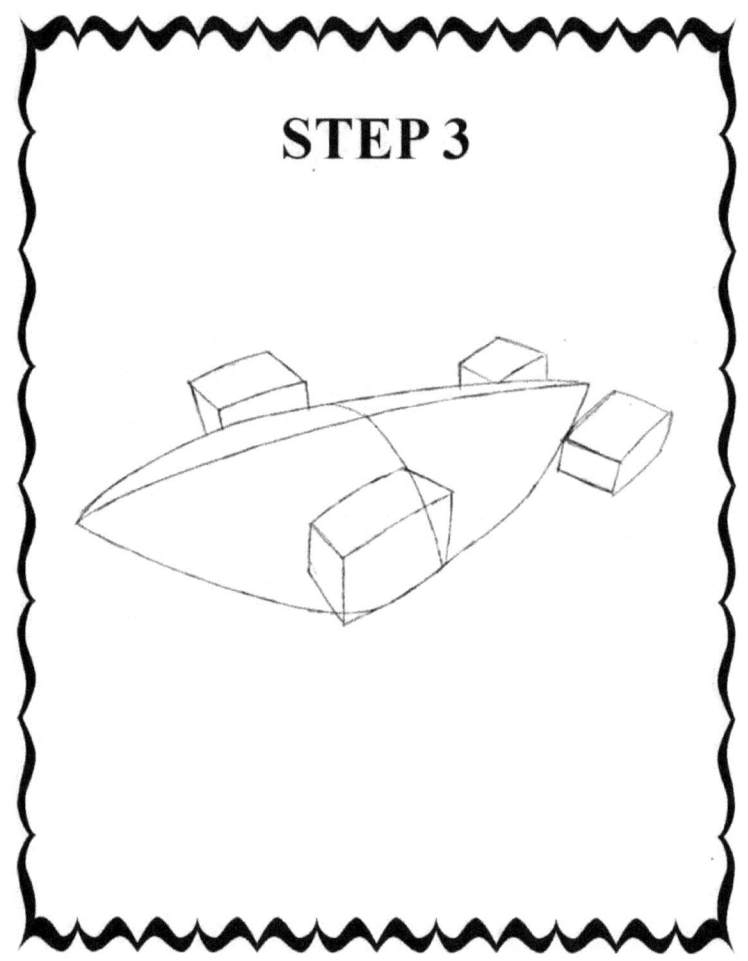

STEP 4

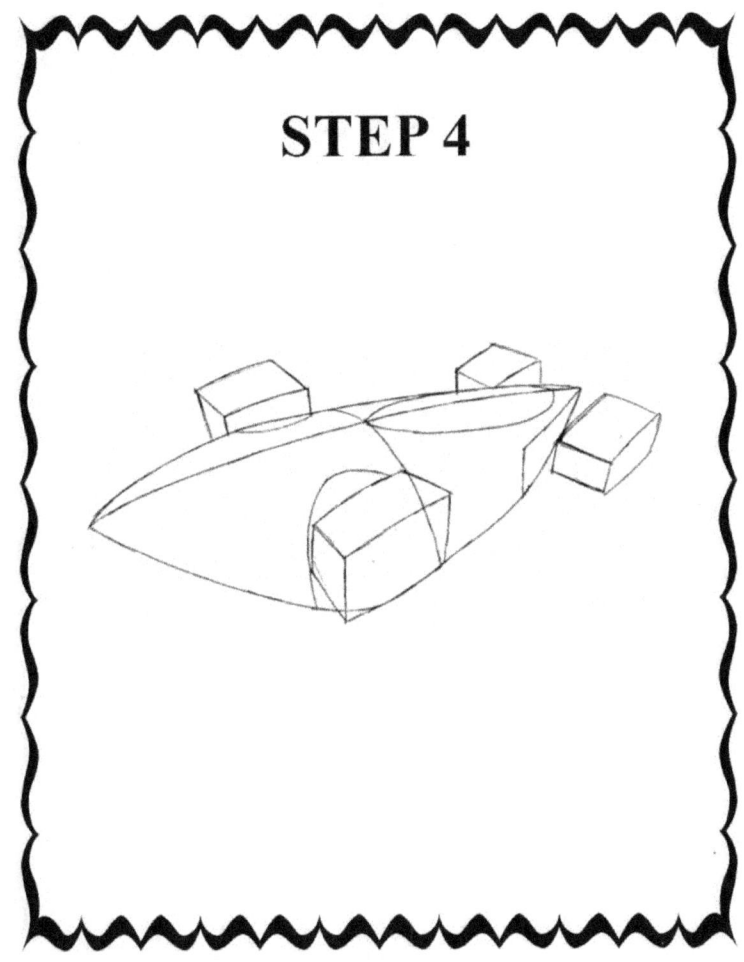

STEP 5

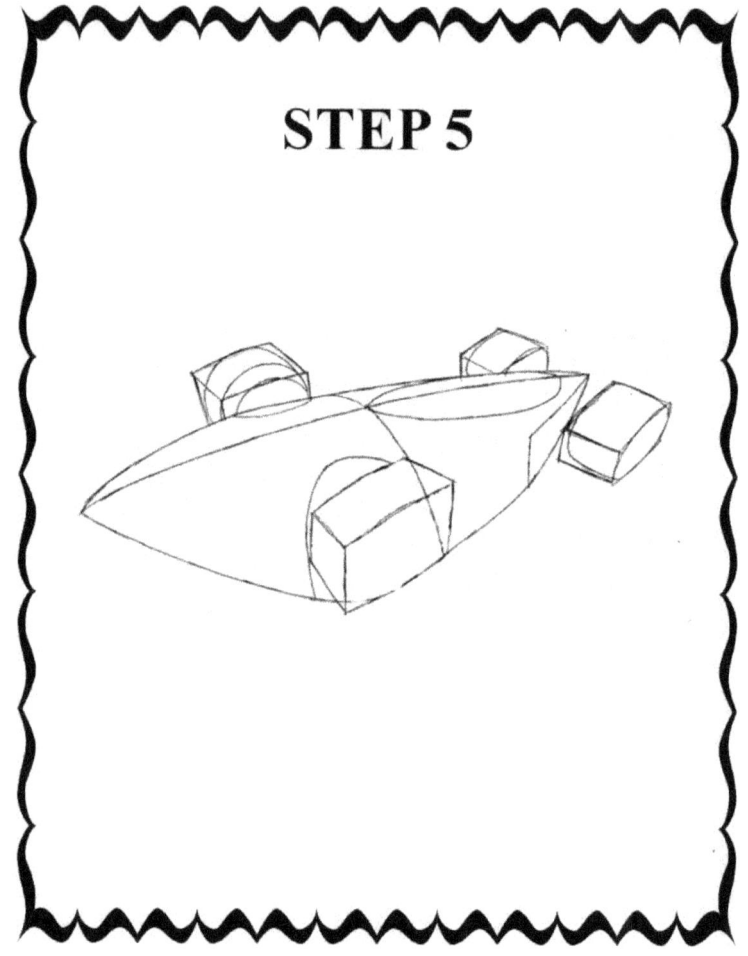

STEP 6

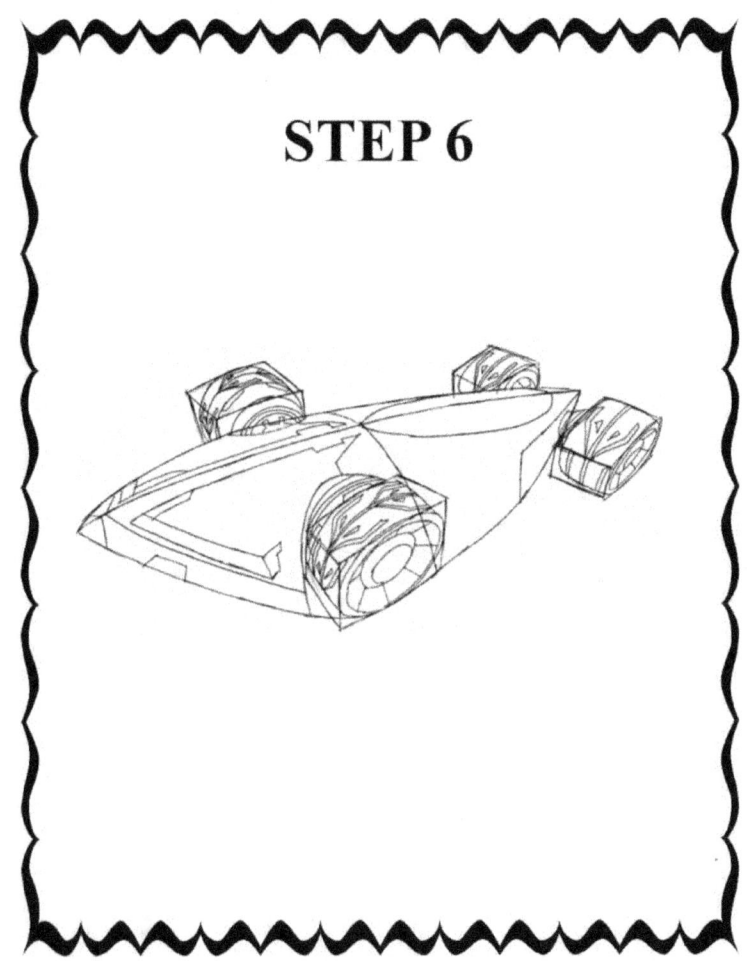

TRAIN

STEP 1

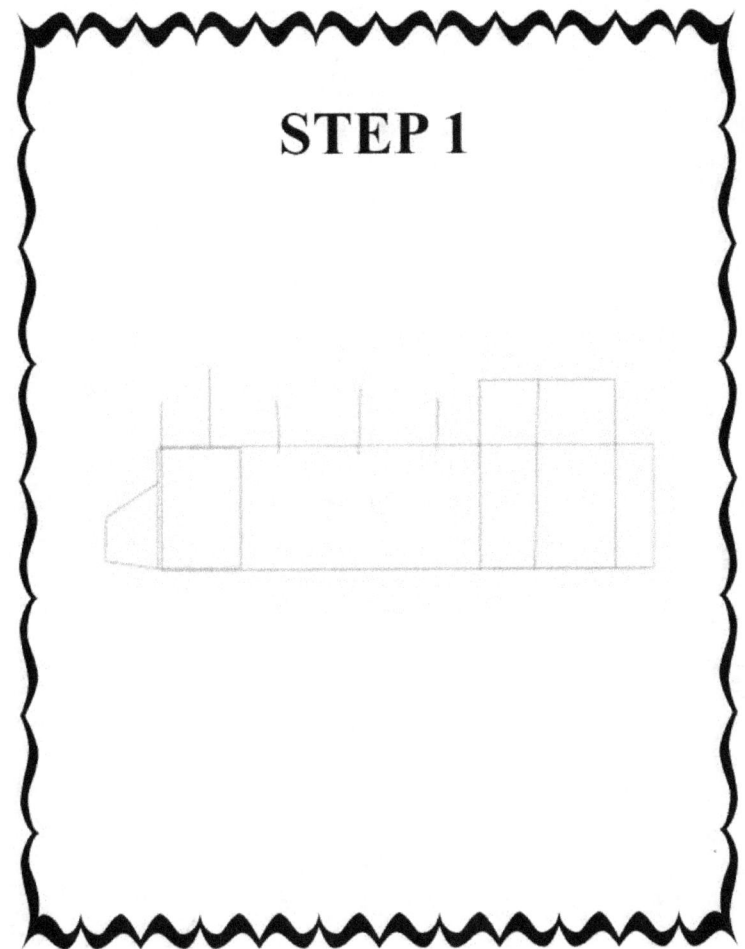

STEP 2

STEP 3

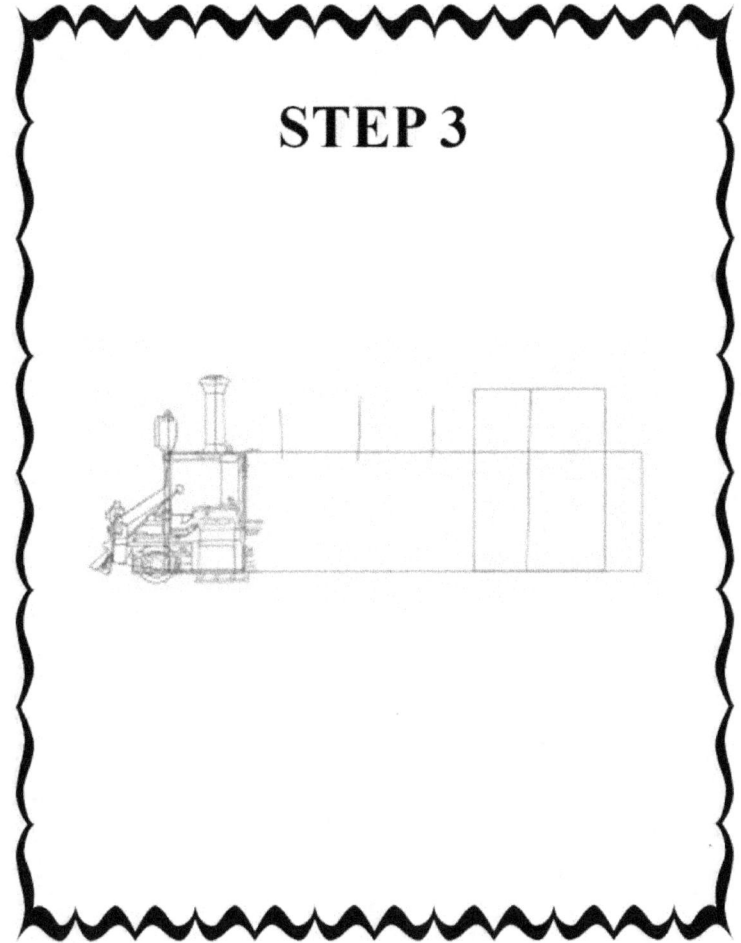

STEP 4

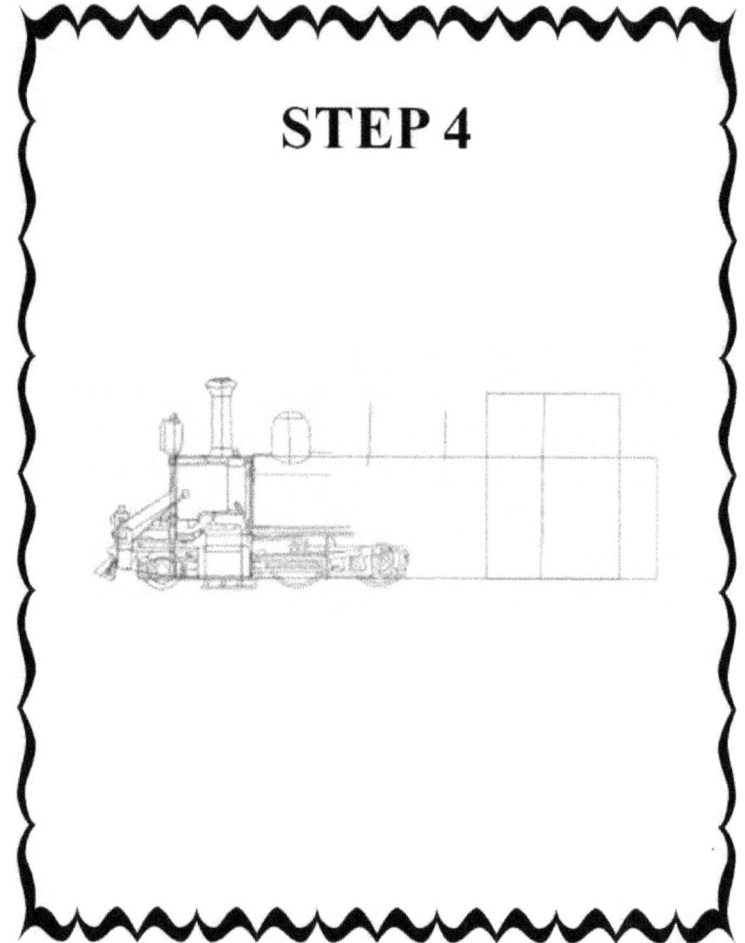

STEP 5

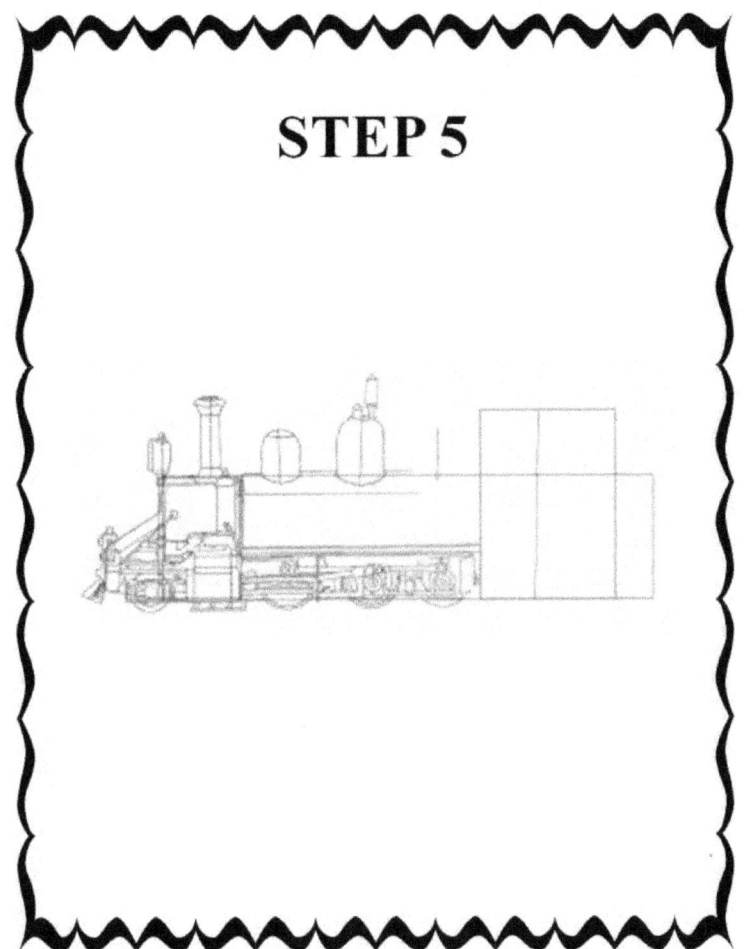

STEP 6

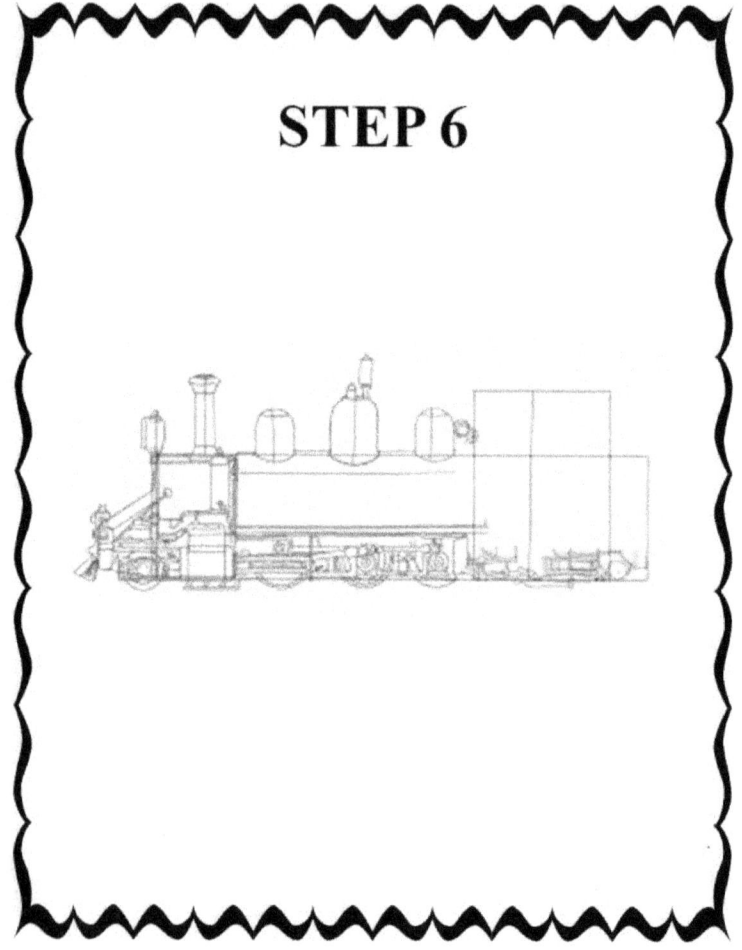

STEP 7

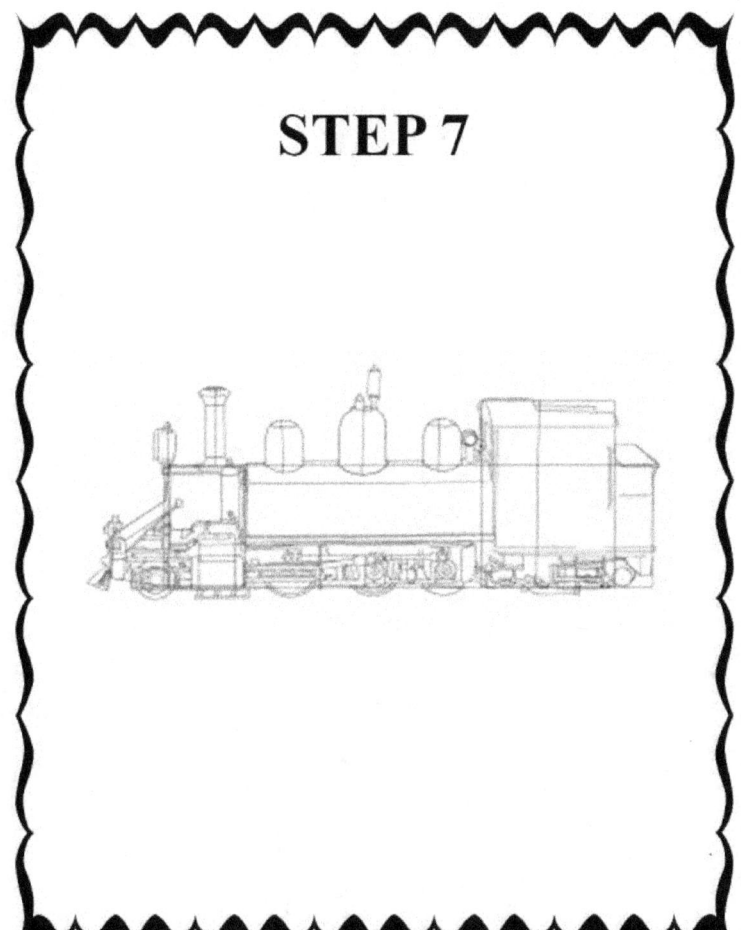

STEP 8

TRUCK

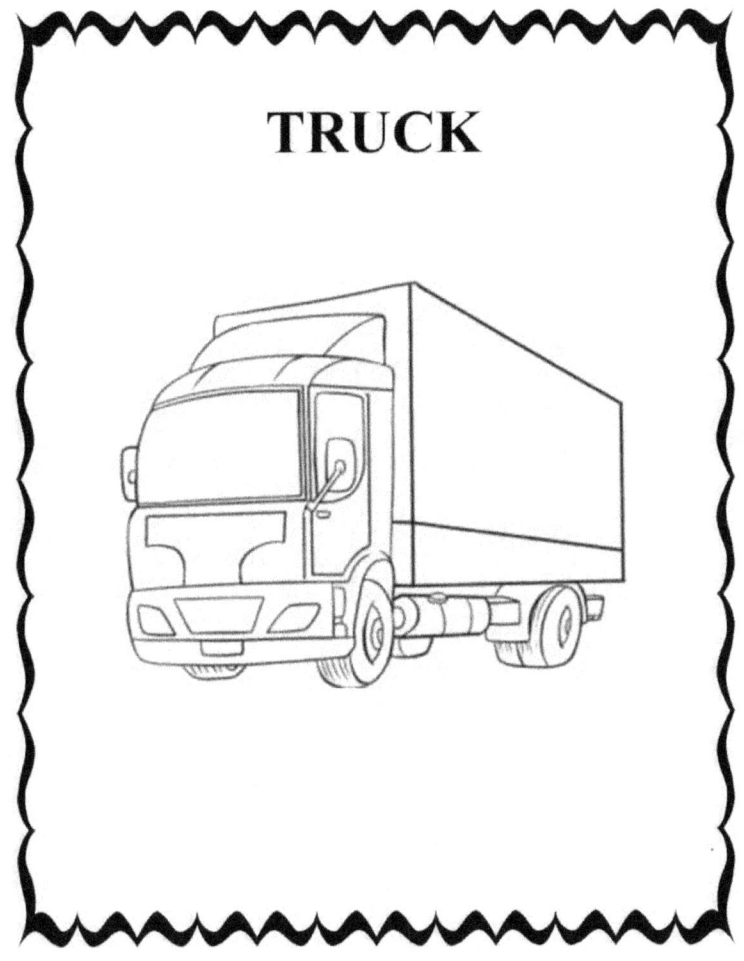

STEP 1

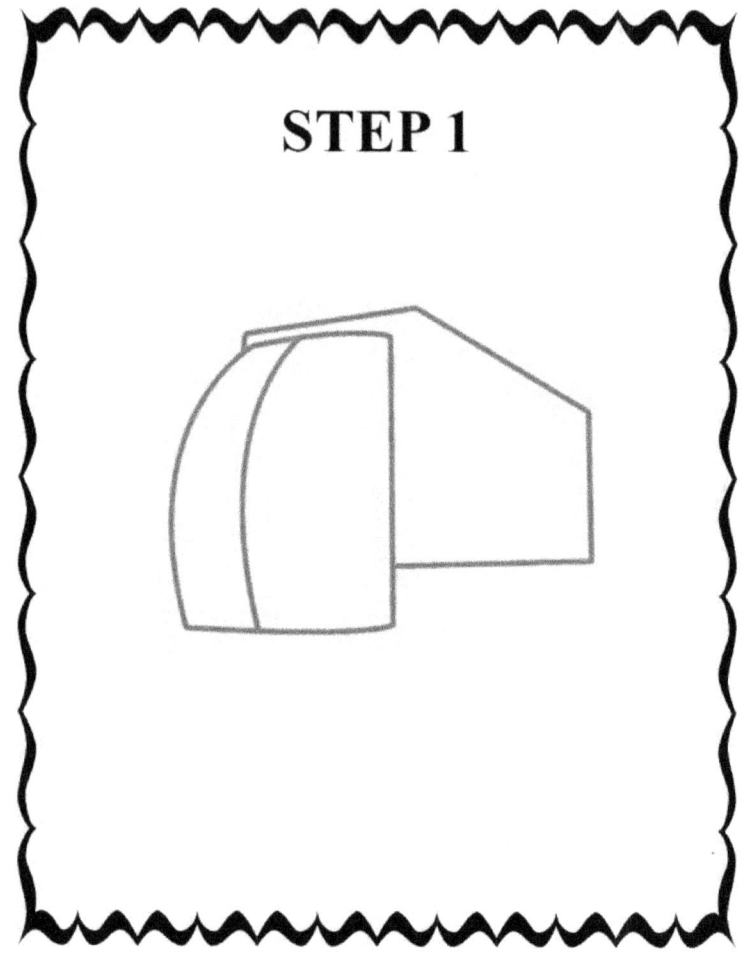

STEP 2

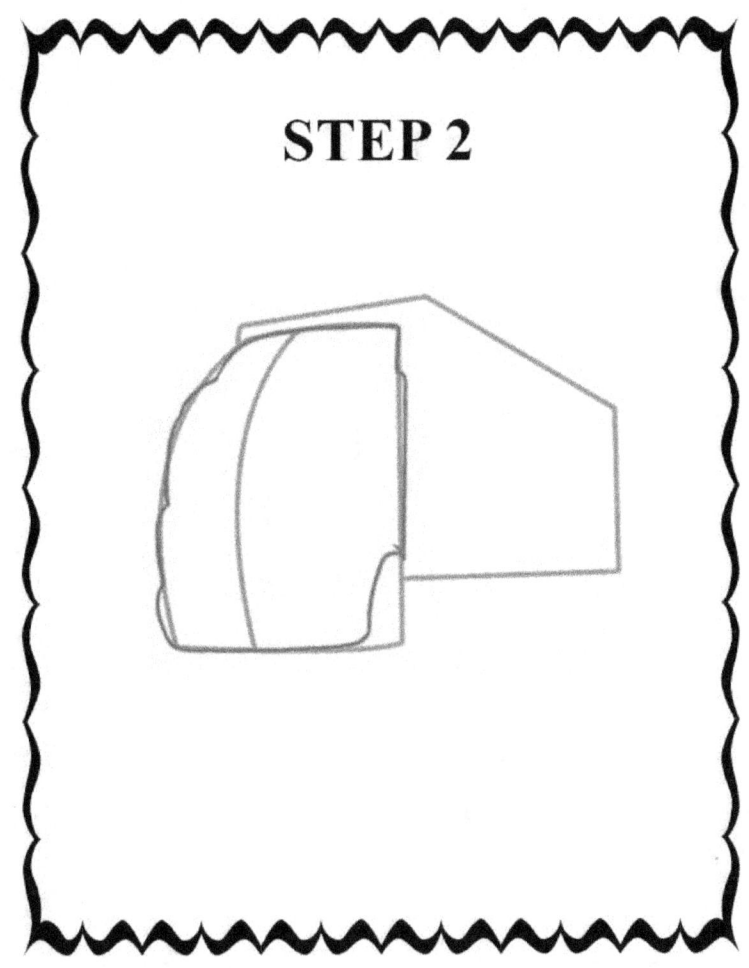

STEP 3

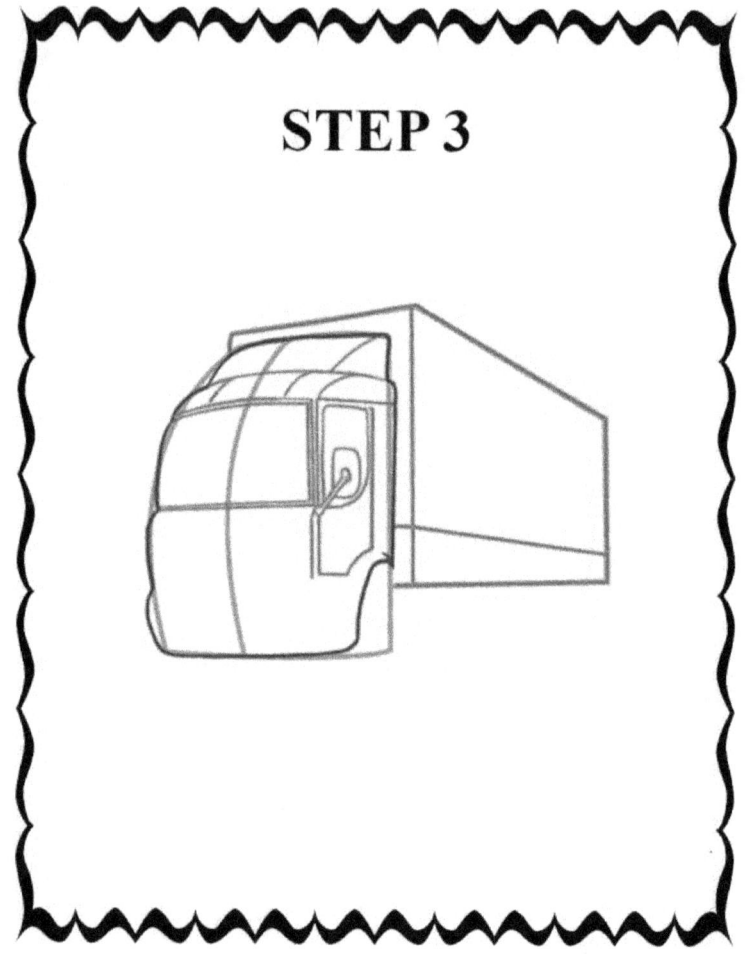

STEP 4

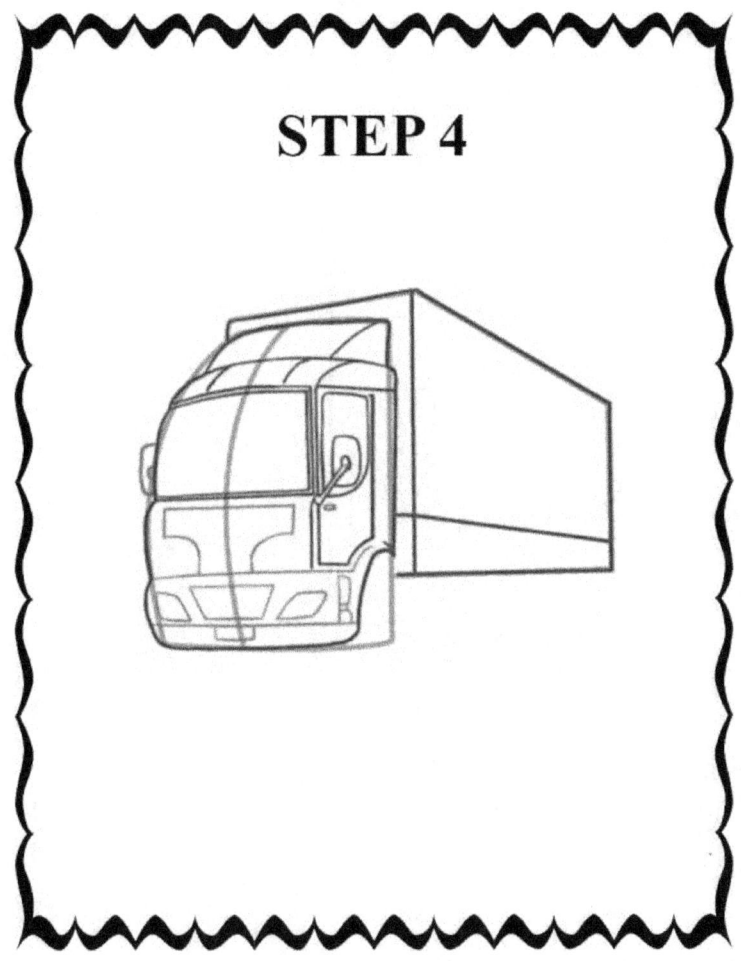

STEP 5

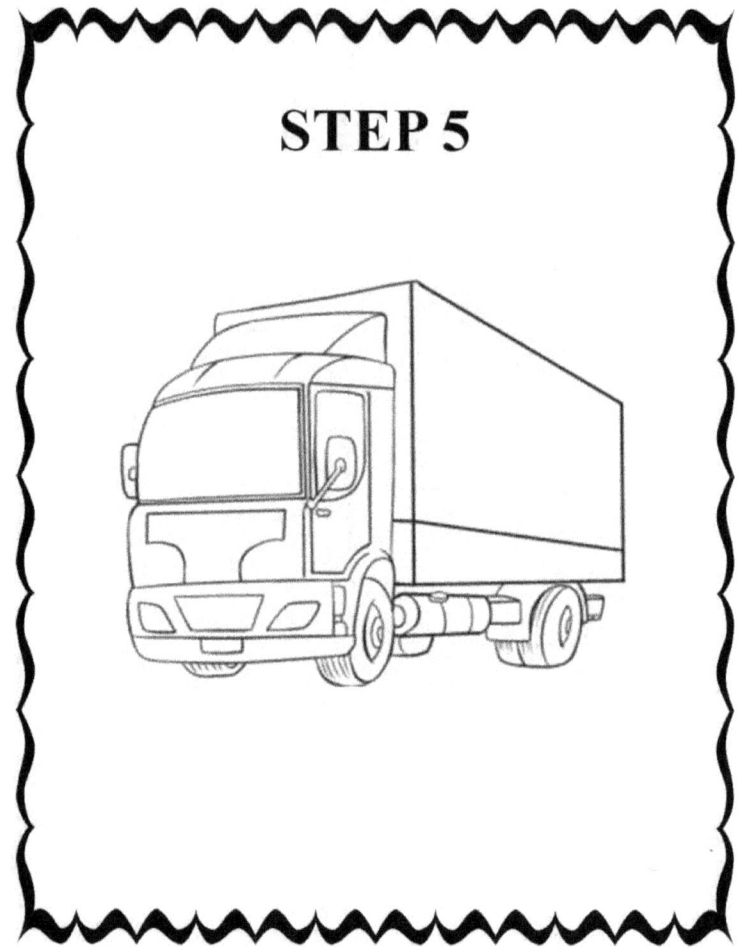

www.ingramcontent.com/pod-product-compliance
Lightning Source LLC
Chambersburg PA
CBHW071648170526
45166CB00003B/1488